ADDISON-WESLEY KIDS 3

An English Course

Michael Walker

Original Music by Bob Schneider

Addison-Wesley Publishing Company

Reading, Massachusetts • Menlo Park, California • New York • Don Mills, Ontario
Wokingham, England • Amsterdam • Bonn • Sydney • Singapore • Tokyo • Madrid • San Juan

A Publication of the World Language Division

Editor-in-Chief: Judith Bittinger
Project Director: Elinor Chamas
Editorial Development: Claire Smith
Production/Manufacturing: James W. Gibbons
Design, Art Direction, and Production: Taurins Design Associates, New York
Cover Art: Cyd Moore

Illustrations: Teresa Anderko 16, 17, 49, 70; Ellen Appleby 7; Susan Avishai 35, 69; Don Baker 63; Yvette Banek 8, 9, 18, 19, 32, 33, 42, 43; Karen Bell 76; Frank Bozzo 52, 53, 54, 55; Maryann Cocca 34, 61, 64, 65; Nancy Didion 24, 25, 40, 41, 68; Mena Dolobowsky 23; Joanna Fabris 77, 78, 79, 80; Ann Iosa 48, 59; Susan Lexa 11, 13, 21, 45, 72, 73; Karen Loccisano 4, 10, 12, 36, 39, 44, 60; Ben Mahan 22, 58; Jan Palmer 5, 46, 47; Diane Paterson 62; John Sandford 6, 14, 37, 38; Dave Sullivan 26, 27, 50, 51, 74, 75; Kurt Vargo 56, 57, 66, 67; John Wallner 71; Marsha Winborn 15

Photographer: Dr. Ronald H. Cohn 28, 29, 30, 31

ISBN 0-201-52129-6
11 12 13 14 15 – BAM – 04 03 02 01 00

Contents

Get Set

Hi. What's your name?
My name is Dan.
What's your name?
Maria. How old are you?
I'm nine. How about you?
I'm ten.

This is Dan.

Hello,
I'm Pat.
Hi. My
name is Bob.

I Know Everyone's Name

This is a nice song.
This is a nice song.
I know everyone's name.
We will get along.
We will get along.
I hope you feel the same.

Where are you going?
I'm going to the moon.
What are you going to do there?
I'm going to **drive a moon buggy!**
1 drive a moon buggy
2 grow plants
3 play basketball
4 collect rocks
5 check the stars
6 repair a rocket
7 build a space station

I am looking for my hat.
You are looking for your dog.
He is looking for his bat.
She is looking for her skate.

It is looking for its bone.
We are looking for our shoes.
You are looking for your socks.
They are looking for their sweaters.

1 All Day Long

1. boys

2. girls

3. crossing guard

4. bus driver

5. bus

6. car

Hi. What's your name?

What's his name?

What's her name?

1. playing

2. talking

3. running

4. sitting

1. movies

2. vegetables

3. books

4. games

5. ice cream

6. fruit

1. dance

2. draw

3. swim

4. skate

5. run

6. read

Conversations

What's your name?

My name is Dorothy Chin.

What's the name of your school?

I go to Cosby School.

What's your address?

My address is 416 Green Street, Los Angeles, California.

What's your phone number?

My phone number is 465-2139.

Make conversations about these people.

1.

Mario Perry
Lake Street School
19 West Avenue
New York City, New York
751-0348

2.

Sally White
John Reagan School
82 River Road
Dallas, Texas
553-6794

Now talk about yourself with a partner.

This is Tom's family.
His father is tall and thin.
His mother is short and pretty.
His sister is chubby.
Tom is just average.

What about Tom's uncle?

This is Kim's family.
Her mother is tall.
Her grandmother is short.
Her brother is thin.
Kim is tall and pretty.

What about Kim's aunt?

1. It is big. It is bigger. It is the biggest!

2. It is small. It is smaller. It is the smallest!

3. It is fast. It is faster. It is the fastest!

Terry was good.
She was third.

Tran was better.
He was second.

Jo was the best!
She was first.

Discovery

Measuring

The marks on this ruler show inches.
There are 12 inches in a foot.

Use a ruler.
How long is your pencil?

How wide is your desk?

Measure around your wrist.
Cut the string.
A friend can help you.

How far is it around your wrist?

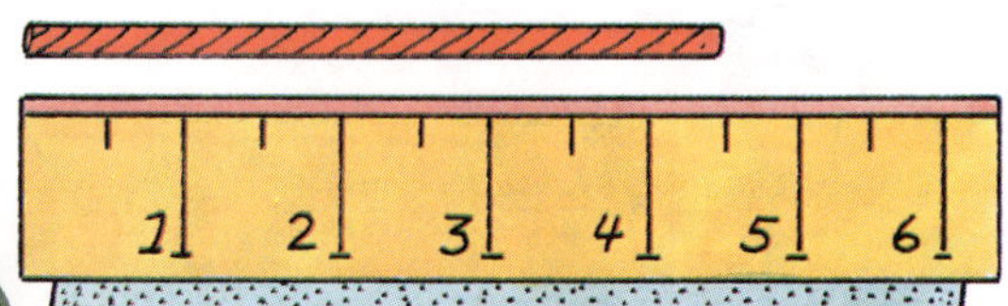

Make a scale.

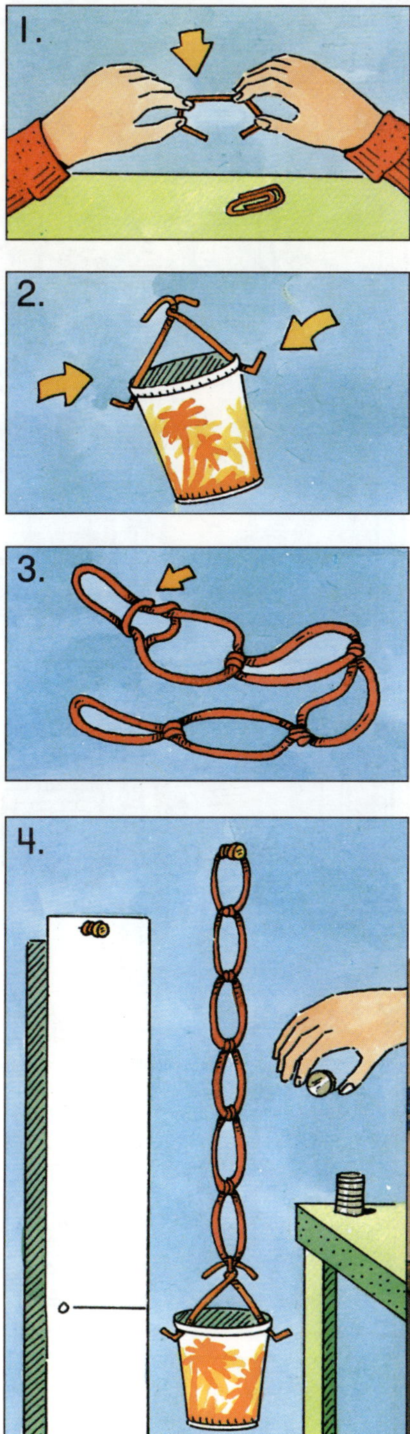

Use your scale to weigh some things.
How heavy are they?

2 At School

1. custodian

2. nurse

3. librarian

4. principal

5. cafeteria worker

6. teacher

Who's that?

What's wrong?

Do you want milk or juice?

1. singing

2. eating

3. writing

4. drawing

Conversations

Make conversations about these families.

1.

2.

Now talk about your family.

How many brothers does she have? She has two brothers.

How many sisters does she have? She has one sister.

Does she have a pet? Yes, she has a bird.

How many aunts does he have? He has three aunts.

How many cousins does he have? He has four cousins.

Does he have a pet? Yes, he has a hamster.

1. When does she have to get up?
She has to get up at 6:00.

2. When do they have to leave?
They have to leave at 7:30.

3.

4.

5.

6.

7.

8.

In my family, we share all the chores. My brother and I have to make our beds.

I have to take out the trash. He has to sweep the floor.

On Saturday, my father always goes to the supermarket. He has to do the grocery shopping.

My mother always goes to the laundromat. She has to do the laundry.

My brother and I stay home. We have to clean our room.

On Sundays, we don't have to do chores. I love Sundays!

Small Talk

DATA BANK

11 eleven
12 twelve
13 thirteen
14 fourteen
15 fifteen
16 sixteen
17 seventeen
18 eighteen
19 nineteen

Say the right thing!

Happy birthday! It's my birthday today.	Thank you. I know. How old are you?
I'm twelve. Here's a present.	Oh, what is it? I hope you like this present.
Open it and find out. Oh, a new game. Thank you.	A red T-shirt! Thanks a lot! You're welcome.
Do you want to play it? I know you like red.	Sure. Yes, red is my favorite color.

Make conversations with your partner.
Begin with these situations.

1. It's your birthday.
   You're ten.
   You get a red hat.
   Red is your favorite color.

2. It's your sister's birthday.
   She's eighteen.
   You give her a blue T-shirt.
   Blue is her favorite color.

Listening

1

a.

b.

c.

2

a.

b.

c.

3

a.

b.

c.

4

a.

b.

c.

Reading

Read carefully. Choose the right picture.

1 This is a car.

a.

b.

c.

2 Her name is Susan.

a.

b.

c.

3 I like to read.

a.

b.

c.

4 He has a pet.

a.

b.

c.

Koko's Kitten

Koko the gorilla was born in a zoo. Dr. Francine Patterson was Koko's trainer and teacher.

Dr. Patterson taught Koko a language. She taught her sign language. You use your hands, arms, face, and body to make signs. These signs stand for words.

Koko learned many words. Dr. Patterson read her stories. Koko liked the story of the three little kittens. They lost their mittens, and their mother was mad. Koko understood. She signed, "mad."

One day, Dr. Patterson asked Koko, "What do you want for your birthday?"

Koko answered, "Cat."

Dr. Patterson showed Koko three kittens. "Which one do you want?" she asked.

Koko pointed to a kitten. The kitten didn't have a tail.

"That," Koko signed.

The kitten looked like a ball to Koko. So she named the kitten "All Ball." Koko called her kitten "Ball" for short.

Koko was a very good mother. She combed and petted Ball. She played games with Ball. She tickled him and blew in his face.

Koko liked to talk about her kitten.

"Soft, good cat, cat," she signed.

"Koko love Ball."

3 Neighbors

1. bathroom

2. bedroom

3. kitchen

4. living room

5. yard

6. basement

I was in the yard.

I was in the bathroom.

I was in the basement.

I was in the hall.

1. washing the car

2. taking a bath

3. doing the laundry

4. painting the wall

When I got home last night, here's what was happening.

Karen was at the beach last Saturday. She was swimming and playing in the ocean. Her father was reading a book. Her mother was playing with the dog. Her baby brother was sleeping.

Sam was at the park last Sunday. He was running on the bike path. His friend was riding his bike. A man was selling hot dogs. A woman was painting a picture.

Conversations

Is your best friend a boy or a girl?

A girl.

What's her first name?

Her first name is Rosita.

What's her last name?

Her last name is Perez.

Is she older or younger than you?

She's older.

How old is she?

She's eleven.

What do you like to do together?

We like to play soccer and we like to dance.

Make conversations about these people.

1. Bob Parker is thirteen.
   He's younger than you.
   You listen to tapes and
   play basketball together.

2. Alice Green is ten.
   She's older than you.
   You roller-skate and
   collect postcards together.

Now talk about your own best friend.

Do the Dog Walk!

When I was a little puppy,
I'd play and play and play;
Now I am a big, big dog,
And this is what I say.

Arf, arf—do the dog talk!
Arf, arf—do the dog walk!
Arf, arf—do the dog talk!
Arf, arf—do the dog walk!

Meow, meow—do the  talk!

Quack, quack—do the  talk!

Ribbet, ribbet—do the  talk!

Lightning

One	Many
1. boy	boys
2. girl	girls
3. hat	hats
4. kite	kites
5. monkey	monkeys
6. box	boxes
7. bus	buses
8. cage	cages
9. dish	dishes
10. glass	glasses
11. baby	babies
12. knife	knives
13. sheep	sheep
14. tooth	teeth
15. foot	feet
16. man	men
17. woman	women
18. child	children

Work with your partner.
Take turns telling how many you see.

Your Bones

This picture shows the bones in your body.
You have three bones in each leg.
Feel the top bone in your leg.
This is the longest bone in your body.

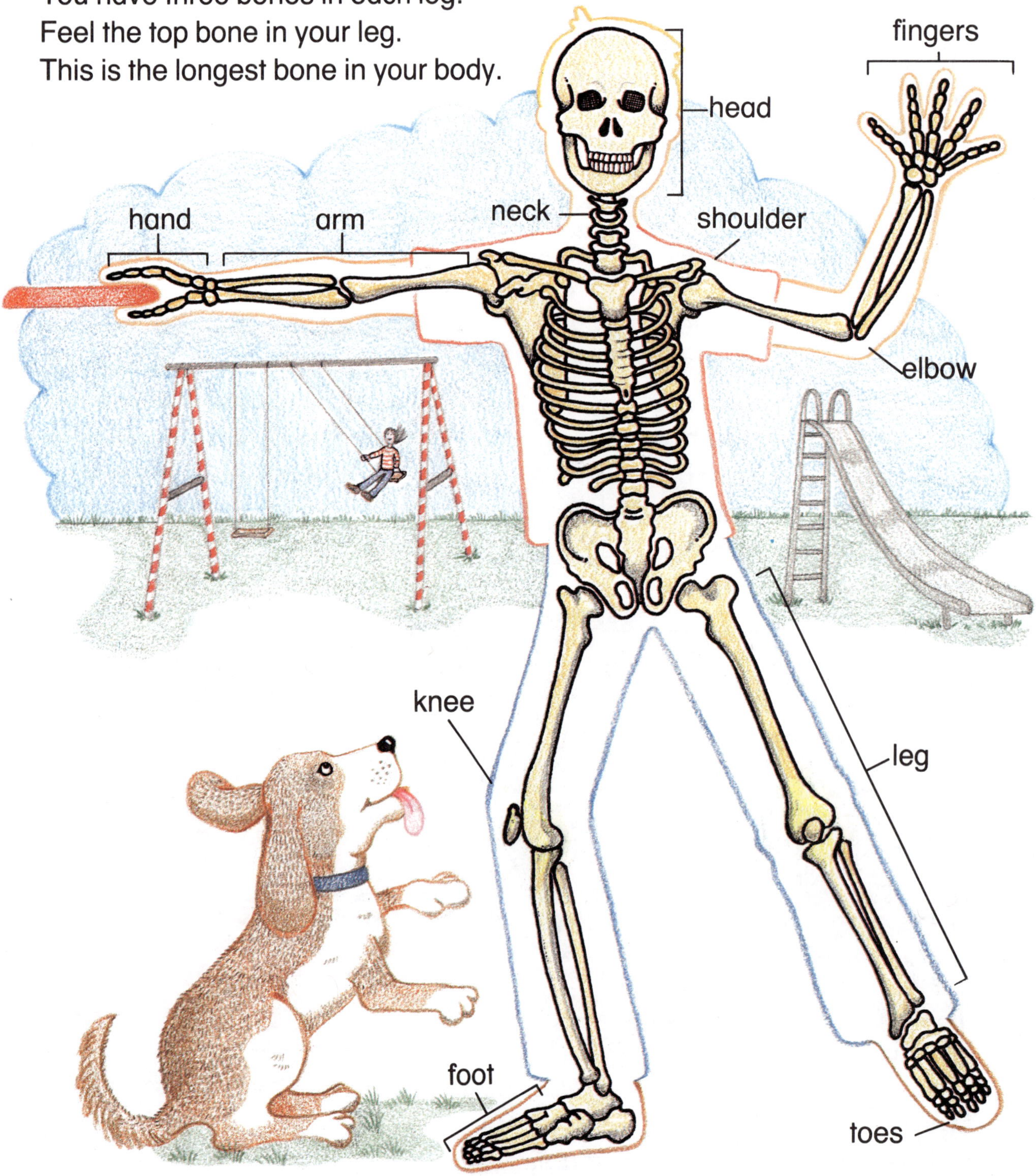

Your Heart

Your heart is a muscle.
Your heart beats all day and all night.
When you move, your heart beats faster.

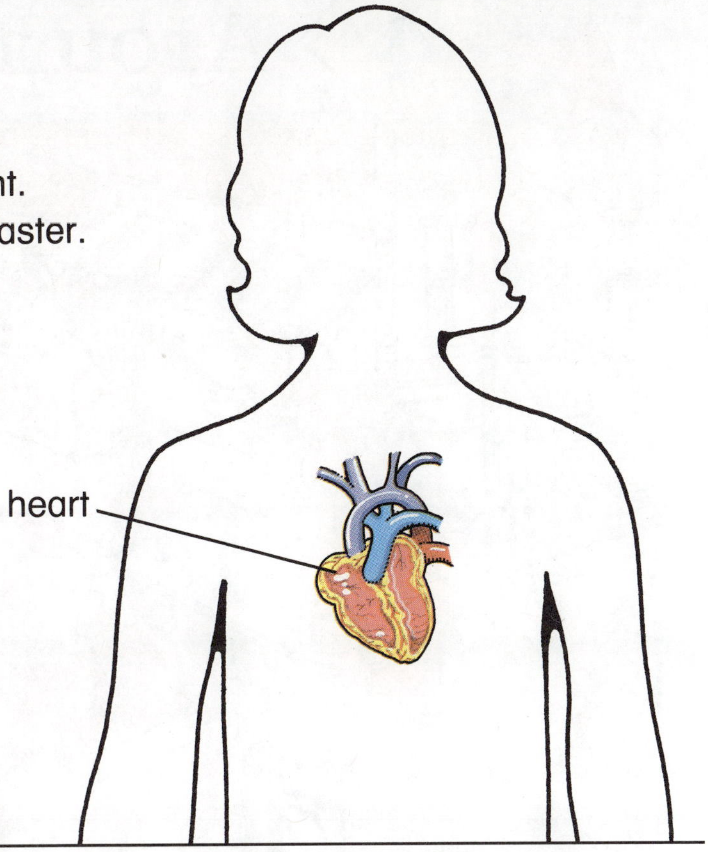

Put your fingers on your neck.
Count your heartbeats for half a minute.
Now jump 30 times.
Count your heartbeats again.

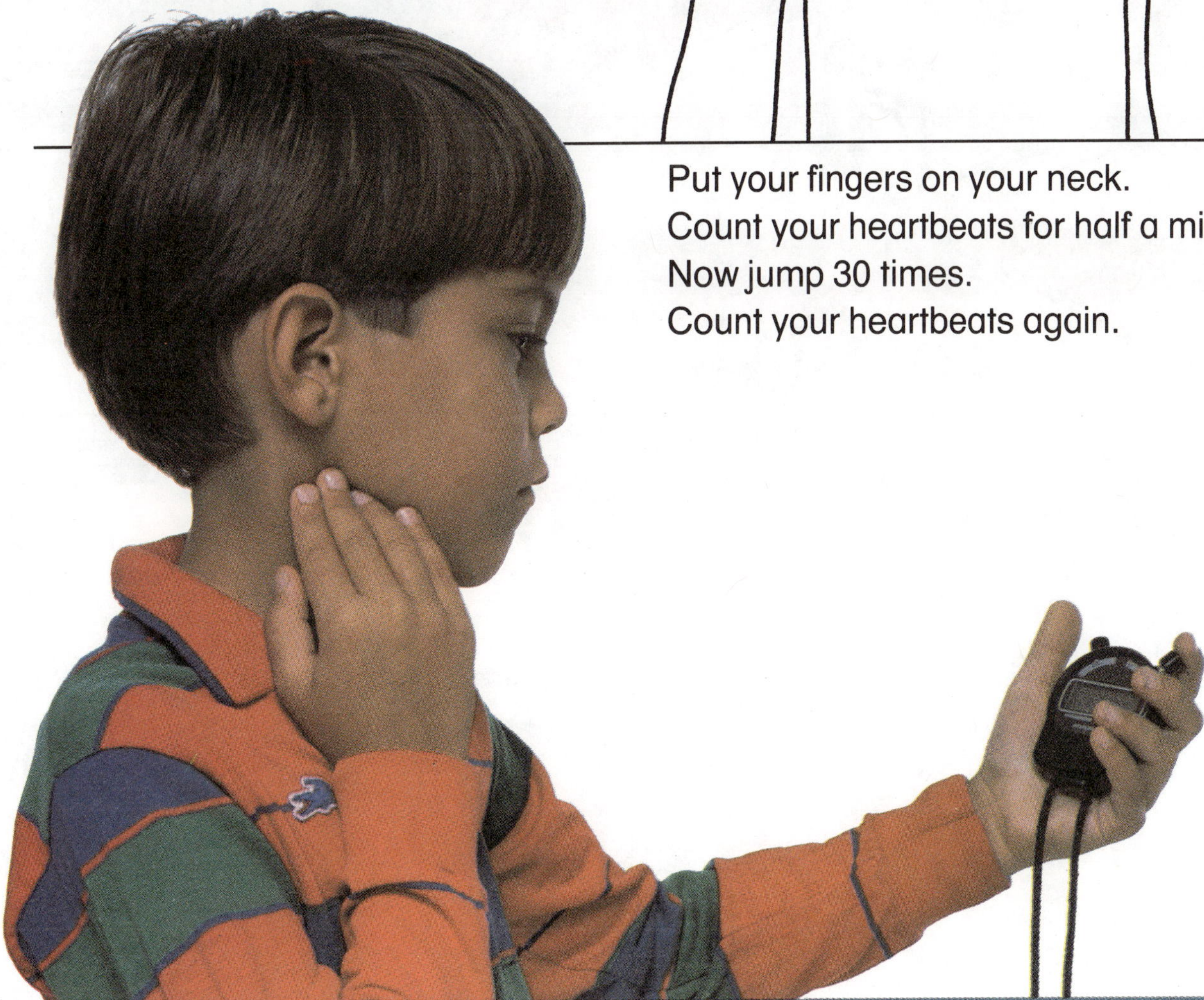

4 Around Town

1. mail carrier

2. barber

3. police officer

4. firefighter

5. bus driver

6. trash collector

When does it start?

How much does it cost?

Where does it stop?

1. delivers

2. sells

3. repairs

4. collects

Conversations

Make conversations about these people.

1. Karen is interested in painting.
   She paints animals.
   She collects dolls.
   She wants to be a pilot.

2. Aki is interested in sports.
   He plays baseball.
   He collects baseball cards.
   He wants to be a teacher.

Now talk about yourself.

1. He works in a restaurant.
   After work, he likes to play hockey.
   He has his skates and a helmet.

2. She works in a bank.
   After work, she likes to jog.
   She has her running shoes
   and a towel.

3. He works in a library.
   After work, he likes to paint.
   He has his brushes and paints.

4. She works in a gas station.
   After work, she likes to dance.
   She has her tapes and a tape recorder.

5. He works in a factory.
   After work, he likes to play baseball.
   He has his glove and a baseball.

1. He is a farmer.
   He grows corn.
   He has a tractor.

2. She is a photographer.
   She takes photographs.
   She has a camera.

3. artist
   paints pictures
   brushes and paints

4. carpenter
   builds houses
   box of tools

5. factory worker
   makes clothes
   sewing machine

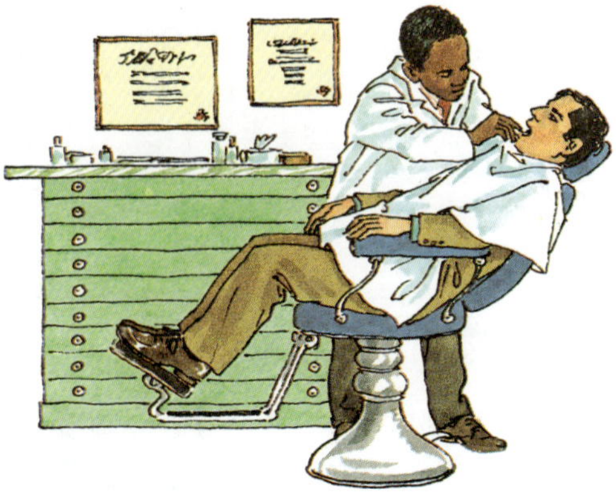

6. dentist
   fixes teeth
   drill

Does he have a truck? . . . . .No, he doesn't.

What does he have? . . . . .He has a horse.

Does she have a saw? . . . . .No, she doesn't.

What does she have? . . . . .She has a hammer.

1. Does she have a hammer?

2. Does he have a brush?

3. Does he have a tractor?

4. Does she have a book?

Small Talk

DATA BANK

Say the right thing!

Pass the bread, please.
More spaghetti?

Here you are.
Yes, thank you.

Thank you. And the butter.
You're welcome.

It's right in front of you.
May I have more salad, too?

Sure. Here it is.
Oh, I see it.

I need a fork, too.
Do you want more fruit?

Yes, please. An apple.
Anything else?

No, thanks.
Here you are.

Make conversations with your partner.
Begin with these situations.

1. Your mom asks if you want more chicken.
   You say yes.
   You also want some bread.
   You also need a knife.

2. You ask your friend to pass the pepper.
   Your friend asks for a fork.
   You need a napkin.
   Your friend wants more salad.

Listening

1

a.

b.

c.

2

a.

b.

c.

3

a.

b.

c.

4

a.

b.

c.

Reading

Read carefully. Choose the right picture.

1

He was in the yard.
He was washing the car.

2

She was washing her hair.
Now she's watching TV.

3

Ken is interested in music.
He collects tapes.

4

Karen likes to paint pictures.
She has brushes and paints.

The Rabbit and the Turnip

It was winter. It was snowing very hard. It was very cold. The animals were out looking for food.

Little Rabbit found two turnips. He gobbled one right up. He wanted the other turnip. Then he thought about his friend Little Donkey.

"Little Donkey is probably hungry, too. I'll take this turnip to him." Little Donkey was not at home. Little Rabbit left the turnip on his doorstep.

Little Donkey came home. He had some potatoes to eat. He was very surprised to see the turnip. "How kind of someone to give me this turnip," he thought.

"Little Sheep is probably hungry, too. I'll take this turnip to her." Little Sheep was not at home. Little Donkey left the turnip on her table.

Little Sheep came home. She had a cabbage to eat. She was very surprised to see the turnip. "How kind of someone to give me this turnip," she thought.

"Little Doe is probably hungry, too. I'll take this turnip to her." Little Doe was not at home. Little Sheep left the turnip on her windowsill.

Little Doe came home. She had some leaves to eat. She was very surprised to see the turnip. "How kind of someone to give me this turnip," she thought.

"Little Rabbit is probably hungry, too. I'll take this turnip to him." Little Rabbit was at home. He was fast asleep. Little Doe left the turnip beside his bed.

Little Rabbit woke up. He was very surprised to see the turnip.
He thought he was dreaming.

"How kind of someone to give me this turnip," he thought. And he gobbled it right up.

5 Busy, Busy, Busy

1. dolphins

2. monsters

3. goats

4. ponies

5. seals

6. sailboats

7. kites

8. space ride

9. train

10. motorboats

Around the track,
Clickety-clack,
The train goes out,
The train comes back.

Where did you stop?

What did you like?

Did she laugh at a funny monkey? . . . . .No, she didn't.

What did she laugh at? . . . . .She laughed at a funny clown.

Did they miss the train? . . . . .No, they didn't.

What did they miss? . . . . .They missed the plane.

1. bake

2. wash

3. lock

4. fix

Last night, my dad rushed home from work. He kissed my mom and said, "You rest. I'll cook dinner. I'll call you when dinner is ready," he promised. I helped him.

He fixed chicken and rice. I washed the lettuce for the salad. He sliced tomatoes and cucumbers. I tossed the salad. I mixed some pudding, too.

Finally, my father said, "Dinner is ready. Come and get it!" Everything looked really good. And you know what? It was good!

What did dad do first?

a. He kissed my mom.

b. He rushed home.

c. He fixed chicken and rice.

Conversations

Make conversations about these people.

1. Kelly's favorites:

red	English
bike	Christmas
carrots	playing the piano

2. Paco's favorites:

green	science
computer game	Thanksgiving
apples	watching football

Now talk about yourself.

1. It's a quarter after one.
It's one fifteen.

2. It's half past one.
It's one thirty.

3. It's a quarter to two.
It's one forty-five.

4. It's two o'clock.

5.

6.

7.

8.

Make conversations with your partner like this:

★ Let's go to the **movies** on **Saturday.**
• Okay. What time do you want to go?
★ At **two thirty.**

Did she play the piano? . . . . No, she didn't.

What did she play? . . . . She played the drums.

Did they climb a tree? . . . . No, they didn't.

What did they climb? . . . . They climbed a ladder.

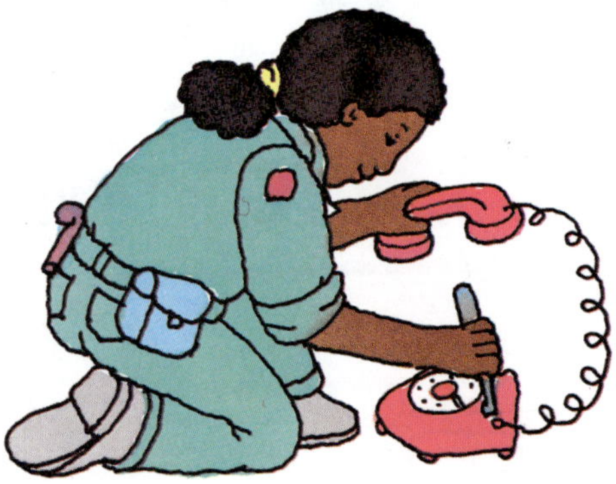

1. repair

2. clean

3. open

4. close

I dreamed I was a rock star. I lived a great life. I traveled across the country. I stayed in the best hotels. I played my guitar for huge crowds. My fans loved me. They cheered and whistled. They listened to my records. They played my video tapes. I was famous!

What is the story mostly about?

a. Fans played his video tapes.

b. He dreamed he was a rock star.

c. Fans listened to his records.

Discovery

Problem Solving

1. Anna collects stamps.
   She had 2 big stamps.
   She has 4 little stamps.
   How many stamps does Anna have in all?

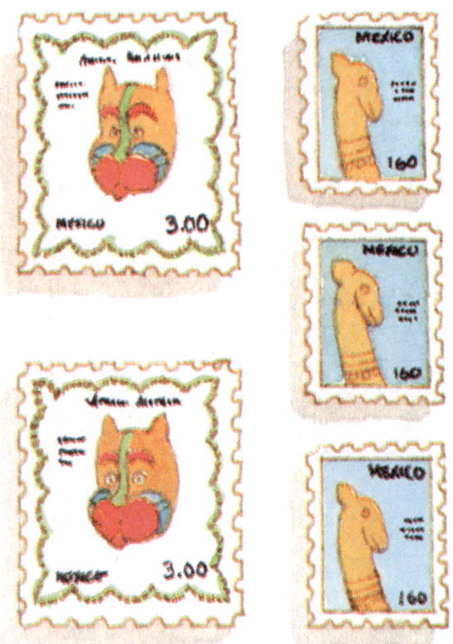

$$\begin{array}{r} 2 \\ +4 \\ \hline 6 \end{array}$$ stamps

2. Joe collects hats.
   Tell the math story.

3. Ben collects stickers.
   Tell the math story.

4. Lisa collects shells.
   Tell the math story.

Reading a Map

Role-play with your partner.

One of you works at the gas station.
One of you asks for directions like this:

★ Excuse me. How do I get to the **bus station?**

● Go **to the stop sign.**
Turn left on Green Road.
The **bus station** is on your **left.**

★ Thank you!

Use some of these words.

Turn left.	Go straight.	Go over the bridge.
Turn right.	Go to the traffic light.	Go over the railroad tracks.

6 Places Near and Far

1. mountains

2. desert

3. ocean

4. lake

5. river

6. bridge

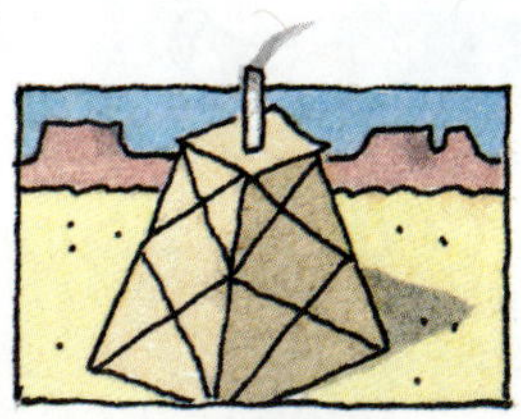

7. oil well

8. monument

9. factory

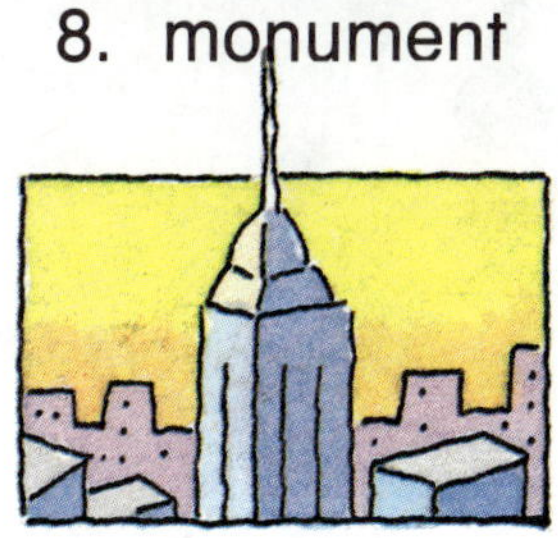

10. skyscraper

Where did they go?

How did they go?

What did they see?

Conversations

Make conversations about these people.

My favorite season is summer.
I like hot, sunny weather.
I go swimming and sailing.

My favorite season is fall.
I like cool, windy weather.
I go bike riding. I play in the leaves.

My favorite season is spring.
I like warm, rainy days.
I plant flowers in my yard.

Now talk about yourself.

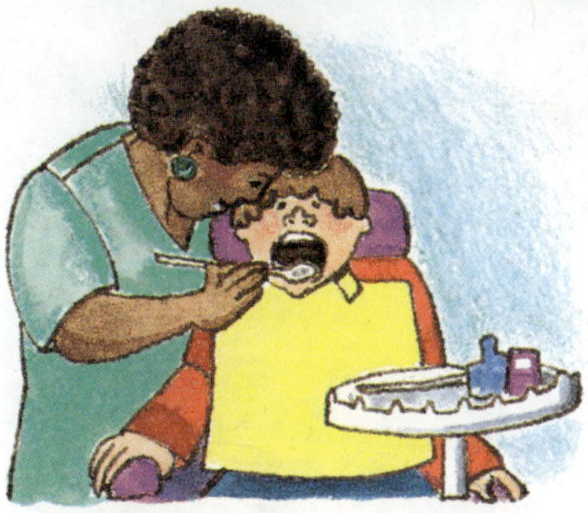

1. go to the dentist

2. deliver papers

3. practice my piano lessons

4. watch my baby sister

5. clean my room

6. go shopping

Did they wait for a train? . . . . No, they didn't.

What did they wait for? . . . . They waited for a bus.

Did they collect records? . . . . No, they didn't.

What did they collect? . . . . They collected stamps.

1. paint

2. lift

3. plant

4. count

She planted some seeds. She weeded the garden. She waited for the corn to grow. She sorted the good corn from the bad corn. She loaded her truck. She painted a sign. She waited for customers. She counted out ears of corn. She collected her money.

1

2

3

4

5

6

7

8

9

What did she do first?

a. She waited for the corn to grow.
b. She painted a sign.
c. She planted some seeds.

Small Talk

DATA BANK

a toothache

a headache

a backache

a bad cough

a sore throat

a cold

Say the right thing!

Good morning. How are you?
Hi. How are you doing?

Fine, thanks. How about you?
Not so good.

Just okay. I still have a cold.
What's the matter?

Well, I hope you feel better soon.
I have a bad cold.

That's too bad. Well, get better.
Thanks. So do I.

See you later.
I'll try.

Make conversations with your partner.
Begin with these situations.

1. Your friend doesn't come to school.
   You call your friend.
   Your friend has a cold.
   You hope your friend will be better soon.

2. You wake up feeling sick.
   Your mom asks you what's the matter.
   You have a stomachache.
   Your mom says she's sorry.

Listening

1

a.

b.

c.

2

a.

b.

c.

3

a.

b.

c.

4

a.

b.

c.

Reading

Look at the picture.
Find the best sentence.

1

a. John missed the bus.
b. John mixed the pudding.
c. John missed the train.

2

a. Ann's favorite color is red.
b. Ann's favorite food is salad.
c. Ann's favorite sport is tennis.

3

a. It's two fifteen.
b. It's two forty-five.
c. It's half past two.

4

a. We played baseball after school.
b. We watched TV for one hour.
c. We played the piano last night.

5

a. My mom had to go shopping.
b. My mom painted a chair.
c. My mom planted some seeds.

The Weekend

Playing on the weekend, playing with my friends.
Playing on the weekend, hope it never ends.
Playing on the weekend, morning, noon or night—
Monday, it is gone.
Tuesday, it is gone.
Wednesday, it is gone.
Thursday, it is gone.
Friday, it is gone.
Monday, Tuesday, Wednesday, Thursday,
    Friday, they're all gone, and
It's the weekend!

Do you love the weekend? Why?
What do you do on the weekend?

How the Moon Got in the Sky

Long ago in Africa there was a wonderful spider named Anansi. Anansi had many adventures.

One night, Anansi the spider was in the forest. He found something strange and beautiful. It was a great circle of light. It was shining brightly. Anansi stared at the light.

"How beautiful!" said Anansi. "I will take it home. I will give it to one of my six sons. But which one?" Anansi couldn't decide.

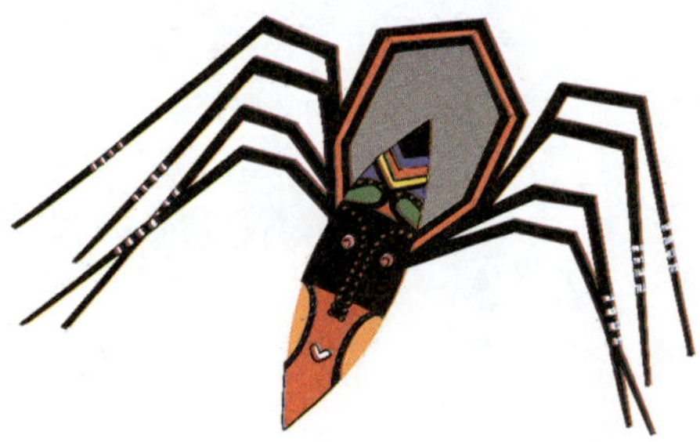

All six sons wanted the beautiful light. "Give it to me," each son said, "Please give it to me." Anansi still couldn't decide.

Anansi called to Nyame,
the God of All Things.
"Nyame, please help
me. Tell me what to do.
I want each of my sons
to be happy."

Nyame was listening.
Nyame was thinking.
Nyame finally decided that
no one person could have
the light. Nyame reached
down and picked up the
beautiful, shiny light.

Nyame threw the light high into the sky.
Everyone could see it.
Everyone could enjoy it.
It was beautiful then, and it is beautiful now.

That is how the moon got in the sky.

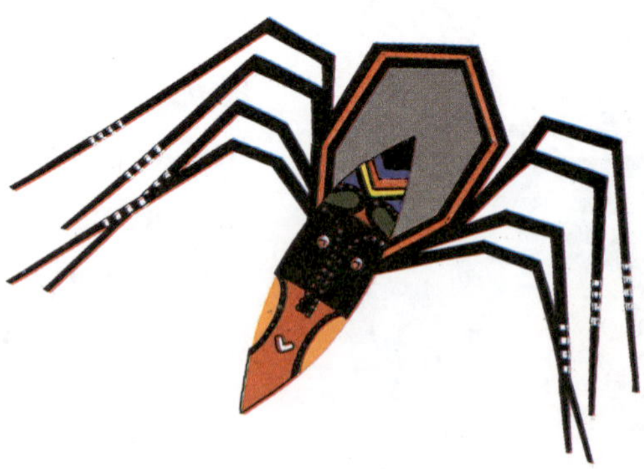